surviving grief

surviving grief

30 questions and answers for a time of loss

A. M. BRADY REINSMITH

JUDSON PRESS
VALLEY FORGE

SURVIVING GRIEF
30 Questions and Answers for a Time of Loss

© 2001 by Judson Press, Valley Forge, PA 19482-0851

The New Testament Scriptures quoted in this volume are taken from *The New Testament in Modern English*, Rev. Ed. Copyright © J. B. Phillips 1972. Used by permission of The Macmillan Company and Geoffrey Bles, Ltd. The psalm quotes are taken from *Psalms for Praying* by Nan Merrill. Copyright © 1996 by Nan Merrill.

Library of Congress Cataloging-in-Publication Data

Reinsmith, A. M. Brady.
    Surviving grief : 30 questions and answers for a time of loss / A.M. Brady Reinsmith.
        p.   cm.
    Includes bibliographical references (p.).
    ISBN 0-8170-1381-4 (pbk. : alk. paper)
    1. Grief—Religious aspects—Christianity—Miscellanea. I. Title.
    BV4905.2.R45 2001
    248.8'66—dc21   00-060326

Printed in the U.S.A.

07 06 05 04 03 02 01

10 9 8 7 6 5 4 3 2 1

This small work is dedicated to the memory of all my deceased loved ones whose lives have been—and continue to be—an inspiration as I travel life's challenging routes.

contents

acknowledgments

My special gratitude goes to Randy Frame and the editorial staff at Judson Press, to my supportive friends at Eastern Baptist Theological Seminary, and to my dear spouse whose love and encouragement have been a significant part of this project. Finally to all my brothers and sisters in our human family who have taught by their personal example that grief is a small pause in the symphony of life, I offer my sincere thanks.

introduction

Death, be not proud, though some
   have called thee
Mighty and dreadful, for thou art not so;
For those whom you think'st
   thou doth overthrow
Die not, poor Death, nor yet canst thou kill me.
One short sleep past, we wake eternally,
And death shall be no more;
   Death thou shalt die.
                —JOHN DONNE

In the tenth poem of his Holy Sonnets, John Donne shares with us his reprimand of death. He speaks to death with words written within the hearts of every spiritually centered person; "death shall be no more."

But in the sunrises and sunsets of our days, the experiences of loss and grief feel too immediate for Truth's consolation. There are no escape routes to take us over, under, or around our intense pain. The quickest way *out* is the most direct way *through* our grief.

As we work our way through the pain, we find that our mourning process is at the same time our healing process. Yes, even in our agony, we are renewed. It may seem strange, yet for those who love God, all things are indeed possible. Our weakness is truly our strength.

In our grief, we know what it means to be brought low. We taste the bitterness of abandonment, anger, and angst. We may even experience a feeling of nothingness as we sit with Job in the middle of a "dung heap."

And then the mystery of resurrection gradually calls us beyond our losses. Little by little, we awaken to the Presence and power within us. The chrysalis of our limitations falls away; renewed, we emerge to share the fullness and promise of the good news—"death shall be no more." We come to see more clearly that loss and grief can do us no lasting harm, that for those who love, all things do in fact work toward the good.

Although this brief book is about surviving the griefs of our life, it is at the same time focused on personal renewal. It is, then, about both surviving and thriving. In Section One a few frequently asked questions about grief, grace, and God are considered. From this overview we move to Sections Two and Three and consider more specific queries about the different kinds of loss and how we might better understand the discomforts of our grief. Coping effectively with our uncomfortable reactions, as well as with the harmful myths about loss that our culture teaches, is the focus of section four. Coming to resolution and recovery involves avoiding "bad advice" and actively working through certain healing tasks; these issues are presented in Section Five. Opening ourselves to personal transformation and renewal in faith brings us to consider the key questions of Section Six. Finally, Section Seven presents several very practical bits of information which include suggestions for helpful books, support groups, personal counseling, and "survivor tips."

I hope that this minivolume of questions and reflections about surviving grief will be used as a handy reference whenever a few practical reminders might be helpful. These pages were not intended to be a definitive statement on the issue of loss and grief. Far from it! Rather this book was conceived in a spirit of gratitude toward all those who have accepted their painful losses and who have courageously and patiently worked through their personal grief. May they be an inspiration to all of us as we try to deal productively with the losses and griefs of our lives.

Like many of my friends and acquaintances who have traveled this life-loss journey, I too have known the pain of loss and grief. At a very early age I lost a dearly loved "parent" to death. Then death almost took me when I was nine years of age. Since then loss has been a familiar companion throughout these challenging decades of my life.

It is my prayer that as each of us grows toward personal and spiritual fulfillment, we will be open to the stories and concerns of others among us who are experiencing the challenges of loss and grief. By our own example of gentle strength and deep compassion, may we reflect the resurrection truth that "death shall be no more."

loss and grief as amazing grace

"Standing alone in the hospital corridor, I tried to absorb the devastating news of my young wife's terminal illness. Our two-and-a-half year marriage was about to be ended by the intrusion of death. At twenty-six years of age, I was to become a widower. Numbness enveloped me. My God remained hidden. Acute pain was my only companion."

—SAM K.

"I myself am the resurrection and
the life," Jesus told her.
"The [person] who believes in me will
live even though he [or she] dies, . . ."
—JOHN 11:25

Almighty and all-loving God, fill me with the trust and faith that Jesus' example gives.

Empower me with your amazing grace so that, like Jesus, I can allow myself the healing experience of spontaneous tears, and that, like Jesus, I too can rejoice in the conviction that the resurrection of my dying loved one is God's promise. Open my heart to the miracle of your healing grace. 🌿✹

how can grief be a grace?

On this side of heaven, there are many challenges and few absolutes. The clever among us may manipulate numbers and dodge taxes, and those with sharp wits and swift maneuvers often bypass the unpleasant tasks of life. However, no one ever escapes the one absolute of all human absolutes. No one ever escapes the experience of loss and grief. Even the virtuous find no immunity against the intrusions of this universal reality, of this pain of loss and grief.

Although each person's experience of loss and grief is so unique that no one else can totally identify with another's cognitive and emotional turmoil, still every human being walks this road sooner or later. While on the one hand, comfort may come from knowing that we are not alone in our grief, on the other hand, discomfort may come from knowing that no one else can appreciate exactly how our loss touches us in body, mind, and spirit. When we feel entrapped by the pain of our isolation and anxiety, when we feel out of the loop of life, then paradoxically, we have the company of countless others, because to be human is to be a griever for all kinds of losses. For whatever consolation it might allow, we are never completely alone in our experience of loss and grief. The whole human race is with us.

For those who maintain a living faith, God remains the primary, though sometimes hidden, support during these periods of intense pain. In itself, pain is not considered to be of any value; rarely is it seen as a gift of grace. But then our ordinary perceptions are not always correct. When we look at pain in general, we know from experience that it invariably tells us that something is wrong, something is off-balance. Physically, a fever alerts us to the fact that bacteria or a virus has invaded our body. Without the fever and the discomfort of its message, the presence of sickness might go unchecked. And so there is survival value in the pain that a fever causes. In a general sense, then, the physical pain that accompanies the burning away of sickness can remind us that the health of the body is being advanced.

By analogy, the pain of loss and grief also carries an important message. It too tells us that things are temporarily out of balance. We feel sick at heart and disconnected from things familiar. We may be unable, because of our great distress, to recognize the deeper message of our pain, the message that says, "You are going through an important change; you are being offered an opportunity for greater personal growth."

Though it is very difficult to accept the pain of loss and grief, we need to do just that. We need to stay for a little while with the pain, knowing that, like the discomfort of fever, and like all things temporal, this too will pass. Eventually we may recognize that God was present all the time. We may even come to know the amazing grace that was hidden in our painful experience of loss and grief.

where is GOD when I grieve?

As we sit alone in the darkness and incomprehensibility of our loss and grief, we might help ourselves by attempting prayerfully to reach out and touch the truth of Scriptures. Perhaps the Emmaus scene might emerge in our mind's eye. We can imagine that we too walk with this Stranger and the companions. Together, we too try to make sense of the most significant loss of all times. We too feel betrayed, confused, fearful, and yes, even desperate! We too listen in the silence of our souls and are instructed. Little by little, we too recognize the possibility of a more encompassing vision, one far beyond our own comprehension. We too are shocked to realize the amazing grace of God's faithful presence. In our loss and grief, we too walk the Emmaus road. And there with us all the time is Jesus, though we may know him not.

Why can't we discern God's presence? Perhaps our inner vision is blurred by the immediacy of our many urgent concerns as well as the distractions of our encompassing pain. The ears of our soul are blocked by the sounds of our own agonizing cries and fearful whispers. We can neither see nor hear the presence of Jesus who walks beside us all the while.

why is it so difficult to feel GOD's presence?

"Pay attention!" How often as youngsters did we hear this pleading command? Parents, teachers, and coaches have all worked toward helping us appreciate the importance of giving our full focus to the task at hand. As adults who have gained some wisdom, we know now how valuable this habit of attention is. We also know now how very difficult it is to maintain a mindful attitude throughout the hours of a normal day. Distractions of all descriptions have a way of pulling our attention hither and yon. During the best of times, to "pay attention" is no easy matter.

Lack of awareness of the Divine Presence during our times of pain and anguish causes even more difficulty. Our human minds are filled with all kinds of "ifs, ands, or maybes." We have all sorts of hopes and fears crowding the mindwaves of our brain. The mental static and noise is deafening. No wonder we are not aware of God's presence. Yet the Divine Presence remains a constant in our lives, even when we are unaware.

In our distractions and fearfulness, in our confusion and anxiety, we have great difficulty feeling God's nearness. We cannot attend fully to the voice of the psalmist who prays, "Love is the strength of my life; Of whom shall I be afraid? Lead me through each fear; Hold my hand as I walk through valleys of doubt each day, That I may know your peace" (Psalm 27). It is our own humanness, our own inability to "pay attention" during our experience of loss and grief that gives us the (wrong) impression that we are alone. In spite of our false ideas, our incorrect conclusions, God is with us always!

do faith-filled persons feel abandoned by GOD?

Assuming that a person of deep faith is periodically exposed to the "slings and arrows" of ordinary experiences—and who among us is not!—then that same person will, at times, feel confused, frightened, and very vulnerable. In practical terms this means that faith-filled persons will certainly be exposed to stress and trauma, and will consequently feel alone, neglected, even abandoned.

According to the men and women of faith who have passed their holy wisdom down through the generations, it is the person of deep faith and spiritual commitment who is especially sensitive to the feeling of pain and abandonment. The psalmist cries out to God, "Why are You so far, abandoning me as I groan in misery? I cry by day, but You do not answer; and by night, but I find no rest" (Psalm 22). Jesus himself cried out in his agony and asked his Abba, "Why have You forsaken me?"

A deep and abiding faith in God does not exempt the spirit-filled person from the "downers" of the human condition. When one is physically injured, the pain of a sprained ankle, broken wrist, or surgical incision is keenly felt. When emotional confusion finds its way into one's life, discomfort also results. When deep trauma makes itself present, an individual then knows the meaning of terror and abandonment. No one is exempted; pain is the price paid for being completely human, for being fully alive, for being spiritually sensitive.

And so, feelings of depression and doubt, of aloneness, abandonment, and emptiness are not necessarily indications of any lack of faith. In fact, they could possibly (but not always) be signs of our spiritual maturity. We still wonder: What to do? This is a real concern. In our feelings of confusion we again join the psalmist and pray to our loving God, "Lead me through each fear; Hold my hand as I walk through valleys of doubt each day, That I may know your peace" (Psalm 27).

SECTION TWO

kinds of
loss and grief

"My baby was cut down at age six. Having a four year old didn't make life easier. I had nightmares—even in the daytime. Daryn was on his way back from the corner deli when a stray bullet caught him in the head. Without my God and my many rowhouse neighbors, I'd be a goner."
—DAREEN J.

Love knows no limit to its endurance,
no end to its trust, no fading of
its hope; it can outlast anything.
—1 CORINTHIANS 13:7

Almighty and all-loving God, help me to stand patiently in my terrible pain, knowing that you stand with me. When my life's loss brings this intensive grief, enfold me in the

mystery of your faithfulness, and empower
me with enduring hope in your love. Assure
my heart that you are with me always. 𝑥✽

what does loss look like?

Shortly after her fourth birthday, Jennifer lost her dearest friend, Boo. For as long as she could remember, her little black cat had been a part of her life. Now he was gone. Why did Boo die? Where did he go? Will he come back? Boo's death was the first of many losses that would challenge Jennifer's personal and spiritual development. Through the coming years of her eventful life, she would know many kinds and different intensities of this universal and always painful experience.

During her adolescent years she would face the trauma of her parents' divorce, her mother's decision to move out of state, and her own search for an adult identity. As a young college graduate she would experience the uncertainty of a chosen career as well as the loss of comforting friends and the good times they shared on carefree weekends and study breaks.

Adulthood would bring its own genre of loss experiences: the long hospitalization and eventual death of her dad whom she had idolized since childhood; the realization that her fiancé was the wrong choice of a partner-for-life, and that her dream for a future with him was permanently shattered; the slow demise of her mother as the degenerating effects of Alzheimer's disease gradually destroyed a once vibrant personality.

Along with an increased consciousness of her own limitations and finitude, Jennifer would know intimately the pain of these many and varied forms of loss. To her, loss would look like the death of her kitten, the abandonment of her parents, the uncertainty of her future, the vagueness of her identity, the destruction of her dream, and the degeneration of her mother. From any perspective, Jennifer would see loss wearing many different faces.

what are the different kinds of loss?

Trying to find descriptive labels for the many kinds of loss is not an easy task. But it might help to categorize a few of the more common forms of loss. Although the context within which any loss experience occurs has much to do with the depth of grief one feels, nevertheless, it is fair to suggest that there are both major and minor kinds of loss.

Major losses might include any significant and irreversible loss. The death of a loved one would easily fit into this category, as would experiences of abusive divorce proceedings, permanent physical incapacity, irreparable brain damage, and the like. Minor losses could include what are viewed by most as transient and less consequential types of loss. Here we group the "little losses" of life like children moving to a new school, adolescents missing the love of their life, parents coping with an empty nest syndrome, and senior adults attempting to adapt to the unfamiliar changes of retired life.

To suggest terms like *major* and *minor* should not in any way minimize the importance and necessity of loss and grief resolution. Why? Because no matter what kind of loss one experiences, an essential relational break has occurred. These relational breaks always involve the self, an other, and for the person of faith, one's God. In the relationship with self, lost dreams for the future, lost roles in social circles, and lost abilities because of illness are all examples of losses that are a kind of disconnection with one's self. Relationship with the other could focus on the death of a loved one, on the neglect or betrayal by a spouse, on the change in economic status, or on any number of other losses that affect one's relationship with another person, place, or thing. Even in our closest connection with God we may periodically feel the sting of loss. The feeling of one's nearness to God fades. Nothing seems certain anymore. Our spirit suffers a deep discontent that may be manifest as fear and anxiety. Of all our losses, this receding of God's felt presence can be the most devastating. In the depths of our pain, in the moments of our greatest misery, we know the meaning of Jesus' cry, "My God, why have you forsaken me?"

Each of us has his or her own sad story of loss and grief to tell. Although our experiences of loss are uniquely our own, they still remain, in fundamental ways, similar to the kinds of losses everyone else has. In summary then, several kinds of loss (but not all) might look like:

- the end of a close friendship, of a marriage, of any significant relationship
- a move from familiar neighbors, from treasured customs and beliefs
- a loss of meaningful work, regardless of kind and duration
- a traumatic loss of home due to natural disaster or necessary relocation
- a change in financial security and, consequentially, in lifestyle
- any kind of physical deformity such as loss of leg, or similar insults to the body
- the loss of one's personal or professional dream for the future

what makes a death loss especially painful?

Like many other kinds of loss, death reminds us of our limited ability to control the events of life. It too forces a relational change when we least expect or want it. But a death loss also carries its own unique features.

Death is definitive, irreversible, and personal. No amount of sweet-talk will change the finality of a death loss. Power, prestige, and personal popularity count for nothing. A death loss is a "done deal." Adding to the already deep pain of loss are the relational aspects of the death-loss experience. When death claims a loved one, it claims, at the same time, an essential part of oneself. Although changed, our relationship with the deceased remains an integral part of who we are. Death changes the form of this relationship, but we carry the memory and "presence" of our loved one with us as long as we live. Initially this causes exceeding pain, especially when specific persons and events, everyday happenings, songs and sayings, all these and more, remind us of the finality of death—and at the same time reopen the raw wound of our significant relational loss.

But there is a less immediate and often unacknowledged reason for the acute pain that accompanies every death loss. Whenever the personal history of multiple and unresolved losses (of any kind) echoes down the corridor of one's life, then the death-loss pain can be truly severe. Little losses from which we have not adequately recovered "sleep" in our hearts. When a new loss trauma touches us, the unresolved griefs, like dormant parasites, gradually come awake. Their unannounced presence adds to the "spin we are in," to the excruciating pain of our immediate death loss experience.

what is the most difficult loss to endure?

Because the experience of any loss is uniquely personal, qualitative labels are largely irrelevant. However, most grief counselors agree that the loss of a child is the single most painful loss one can experience. According to the laws of nature, parents should precede their children in death. When this law is violated, the grief pain is beyond description.

It was an uneventful morning in the ER, that is, until a hysterical father ran screaming through the open doors. As he held his dead baby son in his trembling arms, he was inconsolable. When the chaplain reached his side, this father's grief pain was at the breaking point. The fact that he had three other children, that he was a believing Christian, that he had a loving spouse had no soothing effect. This desperate dad was caught between an experience of a traumatic reality and a passionate pain that few ever encounter. In spite of the chaplain's prayerful presence and the sensitive attentions of the medical staff, this man felt absolutely alone, forced to face the future with a part of himself gone forever.

Assessing the pain of any personal loss is not only difficult; it may in fact simply be impossible. In addition to the impact of unresolved early-life losses, other factors such as temperament, health, sensitivity, and family history can also help to determine the intensity and duration of personal grief pain.

Yet while the power of loss is great, the power of recovery is even greater. The real question that faces us is not so much about the quality of loss pain, but rather about a personal decision. "What do I choose to do?" Will I look back on a painful ending and also look forward to a new beginning? Will I accept my terrible loss and re-establish my relationship with my lost loved one in a different, spiritual context? Will I stay in the dis-ease of my pain, or will I move toward self-healing? The choice, after all, is ultimately my own.

SECTION THREE

understanding loss and grief

"Before Joe's death, I tried to meet his home-care needs. But I'm not a nurse and I admit I was often impatient with his on-going demands for all my attention. Now that he is gone, I feel overcome by feelings of sadness, anger, and guilt. I constantly remind myself of all the things I 'should have done' for him."
—NANCY G.

> . . . I give you my own peace and
> my gift is nothing like the peace of
> this world. You must not be distressed
> and you must not be daunted.
> —JOHN 14:27

Almighty and all-loving God, forgive my shortcomings, my uncaring ways, and my impatience toward myself and my lost loved one. Give me the courage to forgive myself and to be open to the peace you want to give me during this time of confusion and grief. I trust in your love which is more powerful than my grief. 🪽✳

how common is grief?
when is it abnormal?

Loss and grief are so common that no person has ever been able to "dodge the bullet." For all of us loss is a fact of life. To be alive is to know the pain of loss. Although this fact may not be much consolation, it can direct us toward a better understanding and appreciation of the human origins of our attachment needs and separation fears. It can bring us to ask, "How did this relational syndrome, this painful experience of loss and grief, begin?"

Looking back into the mists of our human developmental history, we can, without too much difficulty, appreciate the survival benefit of attachment behavior.

Millennia ago personal security depended to a great extent on remaining close to others who nurtured and cared for us. We became closely attached to our caregivers. Separation spelled personal demise. Those genetic and environmental imprints on the human brain did not disappear even as our communal sophistication continued up the spiral of human development. Consequently we are left with a kind of separation anxiety "reflex" that can easily cause frustration and pain as we work to resolve our losses. Even though we no longer face these prehistoric survival dangers, we still (incorrectly) interpret loss as a personal hazard leading to our own destruction. The result of our erroneous and spontaneous perceptions adds to the pain of our loss and grief experiences. In the wake of these loss reflexes, we now tend to interpret any kind of loss as threatening our personal existence. Intellectually we may know we are not personally endangered, yet the old survival imprint remains to cause us much discomfort. However, knowing the genesis of our distress can be the beginning of an effectual loss resolution.

To be healthily attached is a common human characteristic which marks the usual, ordinary, normal kinds of grief. In other words, in most loss and grief situations, the personal pain is deep and the healing process is gradual, but the survivors of the loss experience are sincerely committed to regaining an equilibrium in their lives. However, possessiveness or codependency can mimic healthful attachment while slowly doing its damage. Unhealthy attachment can deprive the grieving person of autonomy and the will to get on with life. The grieving dysfunction usually begins to take hold in childhood or adolescence. If the kinds and intensity of loss trauma entering a sensitive young person's life remain unresolved or if genetic "wiring" goes wrong during the years of adolescent change and development, then the need for grief counseling and personal caring becomes essential for grief recovery. When this emotional holding is not available, the more sensitive among us remain deeply scarred. Subsequent losses are then felt with disproportionate intensity of pain. When these difficulties are not resolved they cause additional losses to become problematical for us and for those in our relational network. As compared to normal grief, these difficulties are identified as complicated grief. At this stage, professional grief counseling can be very beneficial, and even necessary.

how can I better understand my own loss and grief?

It doesn't really matter where one begins examining the issue of loss and grief. What does matter is the realization that loss and grief are facts of life for everyone. Like the air we breathe, they are an integral part of what it means to be alive.

By definition loss and grief denote the discomfort that all human beings experience when a relationship we have valued comes to an end. It may be helpful to realize that: (a) grief is a sign of involvement, and it is the price we each pay for having had a loving commitment to a significant other; (b) uncomfortable experiences of body, mind, and spirit are not unusual during times of loss and grief, and they do not necessarily mean that we are "falling apart at the seams"; (c) there is no exact time frame within which we are expected to be healed of our pain and our personal reactions; however, a general rule of thumb suggests that most individuals need approximately two or three years for emotional balance to return; (d) because certain facets of our personality are defined by our attachments, significant loss can make us feel diminished, devalued, and devastated; (e) when friends and family are unable to identify with our grief, our feelings of loneliness can become compounded; (f) to be a sensitive and caring human being means to be a griever for all kinds of losses.

An essential reminder for many grievers is that loss and grief are normal—though painful—life experiences. Those persons who love deeply, and therefore grieve deeply, are the blessed among us. Because we have experienced relational closeness, we also experience the pain of separation. The up-side of this separation pain is that our personal growth toward a higher level of consciousness, spirituality, and healing becomes a viable option; our opportunity for increased development in mind and spirit becomes a real possibility. This seems to be the logic of nature and of God's creative plan.

how can it be normal to feel so crazy?

Although grief and its many discomforts are the normal result of a loss experience, they hardly ever feel normal. It does not feel normal when unsettling emotions alternate unpredictably with ordinary emotions. When the highs and lows of life become extremely exaggerated, and our perceptions become grossly distorted, the very idea of normality holds more confusion than consolation for the grieving person. Paradoxically, during times of loss and grief, feelings of abnormality are in fact very normal.

"Hearing" the voice of our deceased loved one calling to us is a normal experience during times of mourning, as is "seeing" our deceased loved one driving the car on the road immediately in front of us. Spending a couple of days sitting in a fetal position on the living room sofa is a normal way of working through the pain of loss for a few individuals. Venting one's frustration by kicking the kitchen cabinet doors is not unheard of. Experiencing periods of convulsive crying and screaming can be listed as "normal." Wanting to spend blocks of time alone is also quite normal, especially for less demonstrative personalities.

These so-called "crazy behaviors" are normal because they indicate that the grief is being worked through, that the pain is in the process of being resolved, that healing is taking place. It is only when this coping behavior continues long after a two or three year mourning period that one would need to suspect the possibility of complicated—instead of normal—grieving.

So, contrary to our uninformed logic, it is normal to feel abnormal. It is normal to see and hear "strange things." It is normal to feel that our behavior during this distressful grieving time is "crazy."

what can I do about my feelings of anxiety and anger?

A good first step toward dealing effectively with feelings of fear, guilt, anxiety, anger, and several other painful emotions is simply to accept them. Attempting to hide these emotions from others, as well as from ourselves, leads to feelings of heightened frustration and failure—even to depression and disease. In themselves feelings are neither good nor bad; they just are! Knowing this can be somewhat liberating. When first detected we can closely observe our feelings. Then when we more clearly understand what our feelings are about, we can more readily determine what we choose to do about them.

According to Webster's dictionary, anxiety is defined as a painful or apprehensive uneasiness of mind, usually over an impending or anticipated ill. Definitions can only vaguely suggest the encompassing panic, and even terror, that results when the distress of loss and grief dog our heels at every turn. Words often fail us when we try to describe our feelings of apprehension and dread. Who can appreciate the emotional turmoil that surges within us only to erupt at unexpected times and in inappropriate places? Who has known my pain? Many others have lived through the distress of loss and grief, but no one else has ever known my exact personal experience. Facing these facts about loss and grief brings us to the realization that we are alone in the uniqueness of our pain, and at the same time, we are in solidarity with those countless others who have faced their own feelings of fear, dread, and panic. And initially that is probably the best any of us can do, namely, to face our feelings directly with firmness and with compassion. We are unique in our pain, but we are not alone in the deepest sense of the word. This is a very sober realization. It is also a very empowering one.

In some ways, anger is a more complex emotion. Spontaneous feelings of anger toward our deceased loved one may sometimes flood our thoughts and emotions so intensely that we are shocked. How could we be so angry with our deceased loved one! Then we feel anger toward ourselves because we believe it isn't acceptable to feel anger toward our deceased loved one. And when the anger toward ourselves gets too uncomfortable, we may displace it onto other living loved ones, or we may stuff the anger deep inside ourselves where it eventually can cause all sorts of trouble for us—and for others. Feelings of anger are integral to the grieving process. As with any of our feelings, we need first to accept their presence within us. Then we might choose to listen to our anger. Perhaps it is trying to tell us something significant about ourselves and our lost loved one. Maybe we need to "talk back" to our anger and make peace with our discordant feelings. Whatever the case, we do ourselves a great favor by becoming actively involved in the positive resolution of our angry feelings.

Guilt is another dominant component of grief that can cause problems during the mourning process. Without much hesitation the tyranny of the "shoulds" takes over, and our thinking becomes dominated by self-blame. "I should have been more thoughtful." "I should have said 'I love you' more often." "I should have been more patient." And the "shoulds" go on ad infinitum. Under the influence of grief pain, it is easy to lose our balance. As we reflect on the past, we seem to forget that imperfections are part of the human condition. We need to accept our human limitations, and realize that we are not, in fact, responsible for our loss. There may be residue from the relationship with our deceased loved one that needs to be resolved, but the fact remains—we are not responsible for the death of our loved one!

So what is to be done about these "unacceptable" feelings? Once again, under ordinary circumstances it can be advisable simply to accept their temporary and unwelcome presence, even to "befriend" them. Along with the various other grief symptoms, these feelings too will pass. However, a repeated note of caution: If one is experiencing complicated grief, that is, grief that involves a history of codependency behaviors or other relational dysfunctions, then a professional counselor can be very helpful.

In summary to the challenging question about what to do concerning our distressful feelings, I offer two suggestions: (a) accept uncomfortable feelings without denial or distortion. They are natural even though they feel very distressful. (b) Once they are accepted, begin an inward dialogue with them, and assure them that a temporary welcome is theirs during this grieving time. (For the doubting Thomases among us, I can only say that this recovery task has worked for many of us. It is certainly worth an honest try.) Accepting our feelings, regardless of how uncomfortable they may be, and then allowing those feelings to stay with us for a limited time will help both to give us more control over our healing process and to keep us moving toward loss and grief recovery.

reactions to loss and grief

"When Ben was living, we socialized a lot. Now I don't even know what the word means. Couples with whom we spent Saturday night outings avoid me. Even in-laws and my own family act as though I have the 'plague.' Common sense tells me that I am not to blame, yet experience has me wondering."
—JANE T.

How happy are those who know
what sorrow means, for they will
be given courage and comfort!
—MATTHEW 5:4

Almighty and all-loving God, comfort me during my terrible loneliness. Let the grace of your divine presence encourage me as I try to reinvest in a life without my deceased loved one. Give me patience as I reach out to those who are uncomfortable with my loss and grief. Help me to help them to help me. 𝓍❋

why do others avoid me?

Immediately after a significant loss, whether it be a death, divorce, disability, or any other kind of loss, the world as we ordinarily know it seems changed and more than a bit unreal. Indeed, "the center does not hold." Body, mind, and spirit feel out of sync. Some individuals find that they have either increased or decreased appetites. Others are plagued by any of a large variety of physical symptoms including headaches, backaches, and characteristics of assorted ailments. Still others experience cognitive symptoms such as inability to concentrate or remember, and a firm conviction that "none of this is really happening." Even one's spirit seems to go haywire. The consolations of prayer and communal worship may seem to count for little. Our consuming desire becomes: "Stop the world; I want to get off!" This spontaneous pain and confusion which permeates one's being is not unusual. Just about every grieving person has experienced these kinds of loss reactions in one way or another.

Given our confusion and discomfort during times of loss and grief, it is not surprising that others, including relatives and friends, may feel inclined to avoid us. They want to comfort us, but they don't know what to say or do. Simply "being there" makes them uncomfortable; our Western culture affirms action but not just "being there." So when most individuals have to choose between "wrong if you do" and "wrong if you don't," the choice is unanimously in favor of "don't."

Besides being unsure about how to give comfort to a grieving person, there is another, deeper, reason for avoiding the company of those who mourn. Death is an in-your-face reminder of our finitude. Especially in our present cultural worship of youth, success, and longevity, few if any want to be reminded of death and its certainty. A grieving person has encountered death. That experience is too frightening for many. Consequently, many avoid those who grieve.

what is happening to me during grief?

In her now famous book about loss and grief, Elizabeth Kubler-Ross identifies several stages that the grieving person passes through on the way toward healing. These are not clean-cut points of passage. The mourner may easily revert back to a previous stage temporarily until the healing finally takes hold. Although there is no lock-step order, denial is usually the first feeling that dominates one's thinking and emotions. Perhaps this is nature's way of giving us a little time to prepare for the reality of our loss. We desperately want to turn back the clock for a little more time. "This can't be happening. It's all a bad dream."

Depending on one's temperament, alarm may result in a "take charge" position or, at the other extreme, an "I can't think at all" attitude. Often one seems to do a bit of both while admitting to an overall feeling of numbness. Some persons cry a lot; others hardly at all; most do both, almost as if their emotions were on automatic pilot. Without any warning the tear ducts are turned on, and then, just as suddenly, they are turned off. There are individuals whose confusion is so pervasive that they believe it was no small miracle that brought them through their loss crisis. Maybe this is another example of the miraculous breakthroughs that permeate our daily lives and that we too often take for granted.

After the onslaught of denial, numbness, alarm, fear, confusion, despair, and related responses, the mind and emotions begin to yearn and search for the lost person. Photographs, treasured objects, special cologne and other memorabilia are all used to "reincarnate" a passed presence, to keep the loved one near.

Grieving persons are often sure that they hear their loved one's footsteps on the stairs, or voice humming in the kitchen. Within a few weeks or months, the searching "reflex" diminishes and then finally ends. When we allow ourselves these pining privileges and go with the natural flow of the grieving process, we can anticipate recovery.

To lose a significant person, place, or thing is to lose a part of ourselves. Consequently, we grieve not only for the other, but also for that part of ourselves that has been lost. Grief reactions are so multidimensional and so unique that it is difficult, if not impossible, to describe in simple and concise terms the many facets of this familiar experience. If we were to try to merge the various reactions of loss into one inclusive term, the word of choice might well be depression. Depression is marked by sadness, inactivity, difficulty in thinking and concentrating, and dejection. In brief, life is a drag! When an integral part of ourselves is "permanently" gone, and the wounds of loss are still sore, depression can be a natural state of mind.

During our grief, deep feelings of attachment and love or feelings of relational confusion are being unleashed. This is a difficult but necessary time of emotional adjustment, cognitive acceptance, and renewed investment in life. In a sense grief happens in order to help us regain—or perhaps gain for the first time—a broader, more inclusive perspective on the meaning of our life, and on the precious gift that life is. Grief has its own inimitable way of asking us to look more deeply into the meaning of our personal lives, and to remain aware that love is all. This is part of what happens to us during our grief.

how can myths about loss be harmful?

Imaginary but meaningful stories are often passed on from one generation to the next. These narratives are used by family elders to launch young folks into a higher level of moral consciousness and personal development. Mythical tales are meant to exemplify the wisdom of the ages: generous behavior finds ample reward and happiness, while selfish acts gain only fear and loneliness. In one way or another, these marvelous metaphors hold the wisdom of the ages. Unfortunately, these narratives can become mutated into strange "truths"; they can become sources of hurt instead of healing, of ignorance instead of wisdom, of bondage instead of freedom. Once in awhile, we are kept intellectually, emotionally, and spiritually tied in the caves of darkness by the dragon of ignorance as a result of embracing an ill-formed myth.

Many of these forgettable "myths" are at best sad imitations of wisdom, and at worst dangerous beliefs about the process of grief. The following are a few examples:

1. "Happiness is an indication that we are pleasing to God." It ain't necessarily so! When the pain of loss pierces our hearts we would be more Frankensteinian than healthy if we didn't grieve deeply the loss which has intruded into our lives. We feel exceedingly unhappy because this same intrusion, whether major or minor, has irrevocably changed a part of us. We have good reason to feel unhappy. And since God is the fullness of reason, it is foolish to suggest that we are not pleasing to God in our humanness and sensitivity.

2. "God sends suffering to those whom God especially loves." In our anthropomorphism and misinterpretation we sketch for ourselves a distorted, even sadistic, picture of God. God does not want us to suffer;

Jesus asked to be spared the suffering of crucifixion. To be fully alive automatically means that we will suffer. To be open to the necessity of change is to suffer, for as Teresa of Avila said several centuries ago, "All things are passing; God alone is changeless." Despite the belief of some that suffering is a sign of the select loved ones, wishful thinking doesn't cancel out the perennial truth that God loves each of us unconditionally—with or without suffering.

3. "Material possessions are an impediment to holiness and need not be mourned when lost." Here we have another myth about loss and grief which, like the others, seems at first glance to be believable. But on closer examination, it too is seen to be incorrect; it only has the appearance of right-mindedness. Yes, we do need to mourn the loss of material possessions. Dismissing the earth's gifts as superfluous could be more an indication of poor stewardship than a sign of virtue. When material possessions have been a means of personal and communal growth and development, they are to be valued and appreciated for the gifts of God that, in truth, they are. The psalmist assures us that all of creation praises God (Psalm 148). Yes, all of creation is good!

4. "Losses, including death, are signs of personal failure." This particular myth carries a lot of clout, probably because in our Western culture we are greatly addicted to success that, like beads of mercury, is too slippery to grasp, too difficult to hold. If success means that life allows our wishes, then loss connotes failure. However, if success is defined in broader terms, it suggests that, like the pruning of nature, losses are the necessary "cuttings" mandated by God for our personal and spiritual growth. Success in its real meaning then denotes acceptance of the feelings of emptiness and pain of those losses, in order that a fully developed person may emerge and bear fruit. In this perspective, losses are a means by which we achieve personal success, which is growth; such losses have nothing to do with failure.

5. "Losses in general and death in particular are evil." Since change, loss, and death are built into the plan of nature, and since all of the major world religions define loss as a cause of suffering rather than an example of evil, this myth needs to be revealed for the folly that it is. Most informed persons would agree that in all circumstances and in every situation suffering must be alleviated to the extent possible. Whether the suffering is caused by a significant relational break such as separation, divorce, retirement, or aging, or whether it is caused ultimately by death, healing and release from suffering is the treatment of choice. When these deep and painful losses find connection with a caring other, and that other shares the pain, is instrumental in the healing, and grows personally along with the grieving person, can this experience be called evil? I don't think so!

how does loss affect family relationships?

Loss has a way of compounding the stresses and strains which are endemic to every family. Irrespective of ethnic customs, religious orientation, economic and educational background, the relationships within any family are sorely tried when a loved one is lost. In a blind effort to ease the pain of grief, it is not unusual for family members to lash out at each other with rebukeful words and unfair criticisms. The "loner" or "outsider" of the family may be the easy target of this scapegoating behavior. Perhaps it is the successful daughter, or the independent sibling who falls prey to this negative reaction of a few, or even of several, individuals within a particular family.

If family members are not comfortable sharing their concerns with each other via honest, sensitive, and one-on-one dialogue, then the blame and misunderstandings can escalate to such a high pitch that professional help becomes necessary. However, more often one can expect to find that low-level relational stresses and strains continue for long periods of time, even years, unless the concept of blame is banished from family use, and the loss is finally resolved.

Darlene and her four siblings were thrown into deep mourning when a sudden myocardial infarction ended their dad's life. According to Darlene's story, she had always been close to her father. She favored him in appearance, interests, and talents. During and immediately after the funeral rituals, she bore the brunt of her family's emotional distress. Nothing she suggested or did was appreciated. Everything about her was criticized. She was made to feel like an outsider who skirted the fringes of an exclusive relational system. Many months of work and prayer finally saw the banishment of all blame and the healing power of dialogue and grace.

When families are open to and accepting of the necessities of change and growth, the individual members are often brought more closely together both emotionally and spiritually after their grieving experience. In the final analysis, loss does indeed affect the relationships within a family. Whether the impact of the loss experience proves to be positive or negative depends to a great extent upon each member's ability to remain open to the grace, challenge, and resolution of the family's significant loss.

resolving loss and grief

"Marsha was ready for her death more than I was. After fifty-three years of marriage, I still didn't want her to go. Losing my 'Funny Face' was the most painful experience of my life. Well-meaning friends made matters worse when they assured me that 'time will heal the heart.' Hearing this nonsense was salt in my wounds."
—TOM C.

So when this perishable nature of ours must be wrapped in imperishability, these bodies which are mortal must be wrapped in immortality. So when the perishable is lost in the imperishable, the mortal lost in the immortal, this scripture will come true: "Death is swallowed up in victory."
—1 CORINTHIANS 15:54

Almighty and all-loving God, renew my mind and heart so that I can accept the pain of this significant loss. My deceased loved one remains, as always, an integral part of my life though now in a different way. Turn the pain of my loss into lasting gain as you turned Jesus' Good Friday death into an Easter victory. ✳

how can I help myself to feel better?

To experience loss and grief is normal; it is also very distressful. Successfully managing these painful intrusions into our lives requires our initiative. As in most challenging situations, common sense can go a long way in helping us recover our calm and equilibrium. And common sense suggests that we get to know something about the healing rituals which help recovery.

Few, if any, of us find the stresses of loss and grief pleasant, but modern cultural denial, like salt in an open wound, easily exacerbates our pain. There was a time in decades past when loss was an expected and accepted natural occurrence. One's cultural and family customs provided ritual healing experiences for all those involved in the loss either directly or indirectly. Black armbands, black drapes for house doors, sitting shiva, anniversary markings, and gravesite visits were a few of the ways in which individuals and families were helped through the recovery process. Although the funeral services are still used, other customs are hardly remembered. The result of this cultural change means that we are left to find our own ways of self-healing. Using our creative imagination, as well as sharing ideas with family members, can reveal several possibilities for developing our own meaningful family or communal rituals for remembrance. These rituals are, of course, for our own benefit as grievers even though they seem to be focused on our deceased loved one.

Having a family memorial dinner can be an occasion for recounting favorite stories and humorous incidents in the life of our lost loved one. If she was a gardener, each spring might find a container of special flowers planted in her honor. Or if he was a sports fanatic, several family members and friends might celebrate his remembrance by attending the season's opening game. The possibilities for creating meaningful rituals are almost endless. Again, our deceased loved ones do not need these rituals, but we certainly do.

Attending to our physical needs is another important way to help ourselves feel better. Like any stress, loss can use up our energy reserves very quickly and leave us feeling weak and fatigued. It is important to listen to the body's needs and to satisfy the added requirements for nutrition, rest, and exercise during stressful times. The alternative is lowered immunity defenses and higher susceptibility to disease. For most of us, this alternative is just not acceptable.

So we must be prepared to attend to our self-care needs, especially around the sixth or seventh month of our grieving experience when our physiological defenses might be especially low. When attending to our physical and emotional well-being we might give special attention to personal care suggestions. The following are just a few examples: (a) take time for a luxury bath or a long leisurely shower; (b) arrange for regular periods of exercise either alone or with friends; (c) attend to good dietary habits and drink lots of water; (d) schedule a private or guided retreat at a spirituality center; (e) seek emotional support via church community or a professional grief counselor; (f) use a journal or audio tape for recording your feelings and thoughts about this loss; (g) treat yourself to a body massage by a professional masseur.

Since it helps the healing process, another practice which many of us use is the empty chair technique. We choose a time and place free from intrusion, and we sit opposite an empty chair in which our grieving spirit sits. We talk to ourselves in a compassionately caring way and give ourselves permission to cry for as long as our tears will flow. This can be wonderfully healing. Although talking to an empty chair may feel awkward at first, it can be a good way to show kindness and gentle caring for ourselves. Many have used this self-healing technique and have gained much from the experience.

how can bad advice hurt me?

Bad advice is a little like counterfeit money. Initially it seems valuable, but closer examination reveals the deception. Family and friends mean well, but when they suggest, "don't cry," "keep busy," "don't talk about it," they are, in plain language, giving us bad advice.

Crying is cathartic. Tears heal our inner wounds. When, where, and to what extent we need to cry is our own decision to make. But we do need to give ourselves permission to cry. Keeping busy can be another bit of bad advice, especially if the busy-ness is a way of avoiding the pain and the tasks of mourning. When used as a "drug," activity is as damaging as any other addictive behavior.

The worst advice and most hurtful suggestion is "don't talk about it." Sharing our stories can be a most renewing experience for body, mind, and spirit. And the telling must go on for as long as the healing process is needed. Telling and retelling our story is a therapeutic practice. Let no one deny us this healing grace. In fact according to several spirituality mentors, our stories are "sacramentals"—opportunities for sharing the graces of our experiences no matter how ordinary or extraordinary those experiences might seem to us.

There is no rule for grief recovery that suggests we should follow anyone's bad advice. To answer well-meaning friends with a gracious response can be beneficial to all: "Thank you for your concern, but I prefer to. . . ." As bad as their advice may be, the intentions of our friends are most often good. An honest and carefully worded response can help us to avoid bad advice while helping us to keep good friends.

are there things I **must** do to recover from loss and grief?

Contrary to popular opinion, time of itself does not heal the wounds of loss and grief. Recovery is, to a large extent, a do-it-yourself process. This means that we as grievers must become directly involved in our own healing. In general, there are four primary tasks for us to do. First, we must accept the reality of our loss. As difficult as it may be, we have to acknowledge the definiteness of our relational separation. The physical presence of our deceased loved one is no longer with us. Nothing we can do will change this unwanted part of reality. Our Christian perspective assures us that our relationship has been changed and not destroyed. Consequently, many grievers find a new depth of spiritual relationship with their deceased loved one which was hardly even hoped for until the reality of this loss was fully accepted.

Second, we must open ourselves to the full measure of our grief-pain. Distractions of any kind will not help our hearts to heal. We must stay with the pain and experience it as a small price to pay for having loved another. Depending on the sensitivity of one's neural "wiring" the pain will be more—or less—intense. In any case, it is of no benefit to compare our painful loss experience with that of others. Our experience of grief-pain is not quantifiable. It is simply, uniquely our own!

Third, we must adjust to an environment in which the deceased is missing. If this adjustment calls for doing my own errands, learning the fundamentals of food shopping, entertaining alone on holidays, attending to my own money matters, arranging for vacations alone or with friends, reaching out to others in new and challenging ways, then I must adapt.

The fourth task calls for reinvesting my energy in a productive and meaningful life. Any significant loss can leave us feeling weak and vulnerable. But through our work toward recovery, energy and perspective return. Practical decisions can then be made confidently. Perhaps the house should be sold, or a car needs to be bought. Maybe a part-time or full-time job becomes necessary. Decisions of any magnitude can now at last be made with the reasonable assurance that we are not making a precipitous and dangerous decision; we're now moving toward enhanced well-being.

when is the pain of loss and grief over?

To quote the everyday wisdom of a popular sports character, "It ain't over 'til it's over." In translation we might say that our pain heals in proportion to the effort we put into completing the tasks of mourning. In certain cases of more complicated loss experiences, professional help can be greatly beneficial. But for most of us, we do well to follow the wisdom of our intuition, and the insights of our thoughts.

Several grievers found unexpected relief from their lingering pain by writing letters to their deceased loved-one. At first, this unconventional practice might sound strange. But if it works, use it! Write about your lost hopes, disturbing anger, personal needs, new dreams. Share your heart-felt secrets. Then read them at the gravesite or at other places which hold special and intimate memories for you and your deceased loved one.

Whatever the memorial practice you choose, remember its purpose. Actively grieving the loss of a loved one is the surest way to honor this unique relationship and to enhance one's personal well-being. Gradually, as the weeks, months, and years pass, we enter into a new kind, a deeply spiritual kind of relationship with our deceased loved one. Exactly when this happens, no one can accurately determine. However, the general consensus seems to be that most individuals need approximately two or three years to complete the mourning process.

More directly stated, the pain of loss and grief is over when we have completed our grieving tasks. How long we take or how we go about accomplishing this work will depend, to some extent, upon the context of our loss; the personal history of our loss experiences; the physiological and psychological sensitivity of our personality; the available support of family, friends, and community; our openness to the healing process; and other variables. If there are complications stemming from our relationship with our deceased loved one, we may need to take more than the usual two or three years for recovery. In any case, we should feel no sense of urgency to complete the process. We should be at liberty to take as much time as we need to grieve.

what if I can't get over my loss?

In a very real sense, no one ever gets *completely* over a deeply felt loss. It would be misleading to suggest that life returns to its pre-loss comfort level after we have worked through our grieving tasks. Reality writes a different script. After a significant life-loss, every sensitive and caring survivor carries a permanent love scar. True, life becomes less painful when the loss-wound has healed, but the scar of that wound remains as a sign of our ongoing and faithful love.

When Megan lost her significant other, she was in the prime of her life. Together she and her spouse had planned for the future, even into their retirement years. The trauma of losing Joe so early splintered those treasured dreams and hopes. She was left in "a dark tunnel with no light at the end." After much prayer, patient endurance, and numerous practical decisions, she eventually reached the end of that tunnel and came to enjoy again a fullness of life.

However, even to this day, Megan acknowledges without hesitation that she carries a significant scar from that loss. Twenty-six years later, she still visits Joe's gravesite and offers special memorial prayers on the anniversaries of his birth and death. Is Megan "over" her loss? No! She will always remember the very special love that she and Joe shared, and her stories about that love sustain it as a part of her family's experience.

Will Megan ever be over her loss? No, not in the sense that she will ever forget her loved one, but yes, inasmuch as she has accepted that her beloved partner lives on in her life only in a profoundly spiritual way. In fact, it is more accurate to say that she is over her loss, but not over her love for her deceased spouse.

Unlike Megan, some people have an exceedingly difficult time finding closure after a significant other dies. For as long as she can remember, Janice had an ambivalent relationship with her mother. As a matter of fact, Janice feels she never really had a mother. In her growing-up years, Janice had no maternal confidante like her friends had. Her mother slept the days away on the living-room sofa, leaving Janice to find her way through adolescence on her own. "Depression" was how her father explained her mother's behavior.

Not surprisingly then, when a terminal illness took her mother's life years later, Janice struggled to deal with her conflicting feelings: love—hate, relief—sorrow, gladness—guilt, anger—forgiveness. Only after working through her complicated grief with a professional counselor was Janice able to get beyond her pain. Although she could not change the sad circumstances of her functionally motherless life, with professional help and support from her church family, she was able to change her attitude. She moved beyond her loss toward a broader perspective on life in general and on compassionate love in particular.

living in faith with loss and grief

"The losses and deaths in my life have been definitive experiences for me. They have helped me to better understand and accept my finitude, and to live my life more caringly. Although the aging process gradually blurs the acuteness of my physical sight, my resolved life-losses have helped to enhance my spiritual vision."
—MADELINE N.

. . . neither what happens today nor what may happen tomorrow, neither a power from on high nor a power from below, nor anything else in God's whole world has any power to separate us from the love of God. . . .
—ROMANS 8:38–39

Almighty and all-loving God, transform the loss and grief of my life into that holy energy which enables me to remain united with your holy will in all the happenings of my years. Increase my belief that nothing, not even the pain of great loss and intense pain, can separate me from your loving Presence.✗❋

what basic truth is GOD trying to reveal to me?

Among the many meaningful tales of the East, a favorite of those experiencing loss and grief is the imaginary story about Elephant and his friend Mouse. As was his daily afternoon custom, Elephant visited his favorite waterhole for a leisurely swim. There in the coolness of his "pool" he half dozed. Suddenly his friend Mouse appeared in a frenzy of excitement. Screaming and yelling at the top of his lungs, he insisted that Elephant get out of the water immediately, if not sooner. Good-natured Elephant slowly pulled his huge self out of the water and looked gently down at his little frenetic friend, Mouse. "Now what seems to be the problem?" drawled Elephant. Mouse replied spastically and without hesitation, "I just wanted to make sure you weren't wearing my swimsuit!"

The "translation" of this little story suggests that an elephant will sooner fit into the swimsuit of a mouse, than God's way of doing things will fit into our understanding. This tale has helped to bring healing to many confused minds and broken hearts. Whether the loss is complicated, as in the case of an adolescent's suicide, or less complicated, as in the loss of one's dream for the future, the bottom line responses are similar. This little story helps to put things into perspective. The time and energy wasted in self-blame, other-blame, or God-blame can be better used in trying to accept our finitude, and in helping the healing process, irrespective of the kind and context of the loss. God's ways are not always our ways!

We do ourselves a great disservice when we torture ourselves with endless suppositions such as, "Why did God allow this?" Our finite minds can not yet know God's reasons. For now we see only dimly. It is later in the newness of resurrection that we will know fully. So for the present, we do better to let go of our "whys" and accept that God's ways of doing things will remain beyond our limited comprehension.

how does forgiveness affect my own recovery?

When the grief of our losses ties our minds and spirits in tight knots we have great difficulty recognizing the reality of our relationship with our deceased loved one. Too often we tend toward exaggeration. We may become fixated on the positive characteristics of our departed one's behavior. Although this focus is not without merit, we must be careful to avoid idolizing our loved one. In some cases, refusing to acknowledge the deceased's short-comings may be a cover-up for personal relational pain that remains unforgiven. Perhaps hurtful words were exchanged during stressful times of disagreement; the finality of loss came too soon and there was no opportunity for reconciliation.

Or perhaps we had the time, but could find no words to reconcile our differences appropriately. Whatever the case, we are left with hurtful memories that call us to forgiveness.

If the scars of our painful encounters remain vividly imprinted in our memories, we may not be able to forget. But we can, in the spirit of Jesus, forgive. Why forgive? Because forgiveness calls us to reconciliation with ourselves, with our deceased loved one, and with our God. Refusal to forgive others often mirrors a refusal to forgive ourselves. What would we have left if we let go of our anger and forgave ourselves for poor judgment, wrong decisions, thoughtless words? We would have more room for love and peace!

Losses of all kinds and of all times have a way of making us bitter or better. The choice is ours. To choose to let go and to forgive ourselves and our deceased loved ones is to choose recovery. Self-healing involves an attitude of mind and spirit which can let go of hurts and allow the healing power of God's unconditional love to bring us new life and well-being.

Forgiveness is rarely easy. It requires courage and trust manifested in concrete forms. Words alone do not make forgiveness a fact. Because forgiveness is a relational experience, courage is required to see both sides of the painful issue—not only the other's part, but our own part too. Without forgiveness of self, there is only condescension toward the other. Real forgiveness is not afraid to look at the full truth of a hurt and then to let it all go, trusting that God's unconditional love will satisfy our concerns about justice and peace.

how do I pray when I can't pray?

Whatever one's age or circumstances, a significant loss can feel as incapacitating as a full-fisted punch to the solar plexus. It knocks us off-balance and leaves us gasping for life-breath. It has the effect of shock, unreality, confusion, and pain. During these times of intense grief we may feel like the proverbial three monkeys. We want to see no loss, speak of no loss, and hear of no loss. In our confusion and pain we yearn for a simplistic life without challenge and without change. We want to turn the calendar pages back to an earlier time, back to a time that used to be without loss and grief.

Yet breaking through the darkness of our pain are shafts of light called common sense. They remind us that not even one page on the calendar of our lives has ever been loss-free. And in any case, life is a one-way street; there is no turning back. But what a terrible place to be! Gone is our significant other; gone is our confidence; gone is our comfort. Gone too is our sense of having any control of our lives. Like Job we sit in the middle of our emptiness. Even God seems to be gone. Prayer is a tantalizing word. We want to pray, but cannot. Is there any way out of this painful dilemma?

The bad news is: there is no way out, so simply sit in the pain and wait in silence. The good news is: God's unconditional love will eventually break through and heal our battered and bruised hearts. To the question "How do I pray?" come these suggestions:

- Continue to set aside times for prayer and quiet;
- Don't search for many words. If words feel helpful, use very few, even one if possible;
- Sit in the silence and wait patiently;
- During this time of grief, let the passion of Jesus be your unspoken prayer;
- Stay with your tears, confusion, frustration, fears, anger, and other discordant feelings for as long as they remain;
- Let your pain be your heartfelt prayer, and remain enfolded in God's unconditional love.

It is rather commonplace in the work of spiritual growth that individuals will experience a "dark night." During this time we are stripped of all consolations of the spirit and all convictions of our faith. We are reduced to feelings of nothingness so that God can bring us to the fullness of life which is the pearl of great price. Perhaps this inability to pray in the usual ways brings an opportunity. Allowing ourselves to become emptied of our preferences makes room for God's empowering presence. May we be filled to overflowing with this Divine Presence!

what might my living faith look like now?

From a biological standpoint, loss as change is absolutely necessary. Whether we consider the microlevels or the macrolevels of our physiology, to be alive means to be changing. Life necessitates the breakdown (loss) of chemicals in order to build up (gain) new chemicals which assure our physical well-being. Even in the non-physical realm, we must lose our parochial mindset in order to become open to a higher consciousness. Scripture assures us that unless we become as the grain of wheat and lose ourselves, we cannot blossom into new life (Matthew 16:25). The reality of our world—and beyond—calls us to renewal. Yet we persist in our avoidance of those experiences that will enable us to grow beyond our present reality.

Is one indulging in wishful thinking to say that the pain of loss can be a blessing in disguise? To one who has tasted deeply the terrible pain of loss, it feels almost blasphemous to even suggest that any good can come from a devastating loss. And yet the fact is that this is exactly what can happen. When the pain of loss is at its peak of intensity, words are useless at best and counterproductive at worst for describing our agony. However, the truth is that every happening of every day is a grace-gift to those who see with the inner eye of the spirit. For example, among the most spiritually heroic accounts I have come across is the personal experience of a man who lost his wife and two children in an automobile accident. His pain was beyond description and yet as he told his story he shared his conviction that even though he did not deserve to lose three members of his family, he wasn't sure he deserved to have them in the first place.

Our faith tells us that each person is a unique creation. It follows then that our experiences of loss, grief, and healing are also unique. Nevertheless, from the example of the living faith of others, we can gain a deeper appreciation for our own Christian calling. The scriptural account of the walk to Emmaus is more than a post-Easter happening. It is a living reality. Emmaus happens every day. In big ways or small ways, each day brings us change, discomfort, confusion, pain—and opportunities for renewal. As we walk the road of our losses and griefs, our confused minds and hearts try to make some sense out of the apparently senseless happenings. We are fearful and in deep pain as we grope for some kind (any kind) of meaning in our grief. We find little or nothing to console us. We are weary, tired, and frustrated travelers along this life-road. We are annoyed at the unexpected curve-balls that life pitches to us. Even worse, we are in great fear of the terrors hidden in the unknown future. The night of our unknowing and exhaustion forces us to rest, and in our letting go, we find the Divine Presence. God was with us all the time! And God remains with us, always ready to revitalize us with amazing grace so that now we may become more vivid witnesses to the good news of God's unconditional and enduring love.

In the wake of our loss and grief, then, our living faith reflects more clearly the teaching of the Holy Spirit as given through Paul's words: "Don't worry over anything whatever; whenever you pray tell God every detail of your needs in thankful prayer, and the peace of God, which surpasses human understanding, will keep constant guard over your heart and minds as they rest in Christ Jesus" (Philippians 4:6). This is the look of a living faith.

how can loss be an empowering experience?

Many of us want to know the bottom line "survival benefits" of our loss experience. In other words, can we count any real gains in the wake of our pain? It would be a bit Pollyannaish, even disrespectful, to suggest that loss automatically and unilaterally makes us better persons. It doesn't! However, loss does bring us the opportunity to reassess our values, goals, and commitments. Life has a way of lulling us into mediocrity; we too easily find comfort in old routines and in stale customs. We forget to ask relevant questions. A kind of complacency captures us body and soul and renders us somewhat lethargic. Personal growth of mind, emotion, and spirit slow down to a drifting-along pace. Challenge and change become anathema. We opt for a dangerous imitation of security and consider ourselves satisfied.

But Divine Wisdom knows better! In nature's world, little joeys are not meant to remain in the comfort of the mother kangaroo's pouch. There comes a time when they must give up the warmth and security of a baby marsupial's life and live in the more unpredictable and less accommodating environment of Australia's Outback country. Nature does not give the joey a choice. It either leaves the marsupial "pocket" at the appropriate time, or if the joey hesitates too long, the mother's instinct boots it out on its ear. Nature knows the necessities of growth and development; she protects her creatures with a "tough love" that keeps them on course toward the fullness of development.

Up the evolutionary ladder sits God's favored creation: human beings. Like the joeys, we prefer not to matriculate in an unpredictable and not-so-accommodating world. The changes that life's losses force upon us are usually not appreciated and hardly understood. However, unlike the joeys, we have a lot more riding on our willingness to accept change in its many forms.

As Christians we have made a covenant with God, in Christ, not simply to work toward our development as persons, but more, to allow ourselves to be transformed into alter Christi (other Christs). Change in the form of our life-losses is an integral part of this transformational process. Losses of any kind remind us to hold loosely to our earthly treasures, whether they be persons, places, or things.

But loss and grief are simply the more visible tip of the change process. The invisible gifts of grace that undergird the spiritual process of incarnation can fill us only when we are empty of our "stuff." Loss and grief help us to become empty so that we may become full to overflowing with the newness of life in Christ. In this sense, loss can be an empowering experience in our life.

helps for healing loss and grief

"According to my deceased spouse and many friends, I am an 'extrovert's extrovert' which is to say I am always on-the-move. Yet during my time of grief, and in my feeling of helplessness, I somehow was able to take alone time for reflective reading and prayer. A support group and my church community helped me to find my balance again, and now I am almost ready to help other grievers to heal."
—RAY V.

The one who asks will always receive;
the one who is searching will
always find, and the door is opened
to the [person] who knocks.
—LUKE 11:10

*Almighty and all-loving God, guide me as I
explore various ways of getting beyond my
loss and grief. Be the teacher of my heart and
show me how to allow my loss experience to
enrich my spirit so that I might help others to
get beyond their loss and grief.* 🪰✳

what practical things
must I attend to?

When Bob was hospitalized for diabetic
complications, death was not on either his
"agenda" or his wife Betty's. An unexpected
heart attack left not only the pain of losing
Bob, but also the confusion of home man-
agement records, personal finances, and
related paper work for Betty.

Because of the numbness that usually
envelops us during times of loss and grief, it
might be advisable to enlist the services of a
qualified family friend or relative, and/or a
professional to help with the financial man-
agement aspects of our loss experience.
Among the concerns which need attention
are the gathering of important papers and
certificates such as: death certificate, will

and trust documents, bank statements, marriage certificate, real estate deeds, insurance claims, medical insurance, life insurance, retirement funds, and social security benefits. Depending on the complexity of one's life style, the paperwork involved in putting things in order could be formidable. Within some church congregations there are those who minister specifically to grieving persons and who can offer support in making necessary contacts, and various other arrangements which a death loss necessitates. We can help ourselves greatly by reaching out and asking for the help that caring and appropriate others are willing to give.

"But I don't want to bother others" is no excuse for refusing the gifts of support which are ours for the asking during these very difficult weeks of mourning the loss of our loved one. Our neediness gives others the opportunity to help us. This grace becomes a double blessing: (a) it allows others to minister to us, and (b) it deepens our sensitivity and readiness to help other grievers in the future.

In brief, we can greatly help ourselves by acknowledging that we need help during our time of crisis, and by being open to the care and concern that others wish to give us. During the days immediately following our painful loss, we are often numb with shock. This is no time to expect ourselves to make important financial decisions without the good advice of qualified others who are thinking clearly and who are committed to working for our best interests.

what role might my physician play?

Marge had been mourning the death of her husband for close to six months when her adult children noticed that her clothes were beginning to fit her like skin-on-bologna. Marge, who always carried her 140 pounds with dignity, now tips the scales at 170 pounds. The extra weight is not heart-friendly and she is not pleased with her excessive snacking. But she admits that her eating helped to fill the emptiness she has felt since her dear Jon had died. Marge is annoyed with herself because she sees her recent eating habits as an indication of her weakness and lack of faith. What Marge does not see is that her need to care for herself does not indicate any weakness of mind or spirit. Rather, her symptoms suggest that she needs to attend to those normal self-care concerns which surface during times of loss and grief.

One of the most practical decisions we can make during our time of grief is the determination to attend to our own personal health needs. Again, how one goes about implementing a self-care plan depends to a great extent on one's medical history and the complexity of the death loss experience. It is not a sign of weakness or lack of faith to accept from one's family physician a mild medication to be used only during the days immediately following the death of a loved one. Even a brief visit to the doctor's office for some practical stress control advice can be very helpful. The medical professionals who know our health history can make practical suggestions for preventing excessive fatigue, weight loss or gain, tension headaches, and similar stress related symptoms. Taking a little time for self-care up front can save a lot of time in self-recovery later.

how helpful are counselors and support groups?

Karen's forty years of marriage told a sweet and sour story. The onset of her deceased husband's alcohol problem coincided with the birth of their first child. From that point on, they knew "stormy weather." When Ed was diagnosed with Alzheimer's disease, Karen's life became more complicated than she could have imagined. Although she never wavered in her love and care for her spouse, the years of stress took their toll. Ed's death brought a kind of relief; it also brought a complicated grief for Karen.

The mourning process has many different faces. Sometimes it looks relatively simple, and healing begins not too long after the loved one's departure. At other times it takes on a very complicated expression and continues to disrupt our life for a longer than usual duration. When the pain of our grief goes on for too many months, then complicated grief takes control of our thoughts and emotions. When this happens it is in our best interest to consider the benefits of consulting with a professional grief counselor. We can gain insights and support from their expertise. A good counselor can help us to deal productively with our acute pain, our unpredictable feelings, our self-criticism, and our recurring fears. If a support system is needed, connections with the right-fit group can more easily be found via a grief counselor. Choosing the appropriate group, as well as choosing the right counselor may take a little shopping around. Don't hesitate to inquire among church members, medical practitioners, and trusted friends for the names of reputable professional counselors who can walk with you through this difficult time. They can help to make a heavy burden a lot more manageable.

how can books and other publications be helpful?

Connie had always been a very independent person. She still enjoys telling the story of how at an early age she refused to drink her milk from a bottle. She insisted on using a glass like her older sister Debbie. Connie had never lost her do-it-yourself style. So when as a young married woman she faced the untimely loss of her husband in an auto accident, she again chose to take an independent route to recovery.

When the initial grieving rituals were over, and family, friends, and caring others had resumed their own daily routines, Connie found it very difficult to leave her workplace each evening and return to her empty apartment. So she didn't. She went instead to the university library not far from where she lived and found refuge in the "stacks" among the many volumes of psychology, theology, and inspirational books. She found these friendly "word-hoards" enlightening, and supportive as they helped to direct her toward the fullness of healing and well-being.

After all the advice she had been given by concerned others regarding "survivor recovery," Connie especially liked the silence of her books. She browsed among them and took only what she found relevant to her needs. Like a bee taking nectar from flower after flower, she found a sweet strength and gentle healing from each of the books she perused.

Many grievers have followed Connie's example. However, most of us choose to use books in conjunction with other forms of grief healing. Listening to inspirational tapes, and reviewing videos about loss and recovery can also be a great help. Informed funeral directors often maintain a special library of books, videos and cassettes for survivors and their families to use as needed.

There is no set list of materials to fit the recovery needs of all grievers. Each of us has a unique experience of loss. Consequently, we each must pick and choose what best helps us to heal our loss wounds. Competent clerks at any large, well-stocked book store, as well as pastors, counselors, and friends, can offer excellent suggestions about books, videos, and music that can help us during our grieving time. The variety and quantity of offerings on the market may seem endless, so choose those that seem helpful and appropriate for your situation. The following list of books and supportive organizations is not meant to be comprehensive, but I hope it will help grieving persons to become acquainted with the resources that are available for those who mourn.

Anderson, R. S. *Theology, Death, and Dying.* (New York: Basil Blackwell Inc., 1986). For those who prefer a more theological perspective on loss and grief, many insights are given in this excellent book.

Deits, Bob. *Life after Loss.* (Tucson, Ariz.: Fisher Books, LLC, 2000). During the difficult period of loss and grief, an easy-to-read book about emotional recovery can be a precious find. This is that kind of practical, to-the-point, and very helpful book.

Davidson, Glen. *Understanding Mourning.* (Minneapolis: Augsburg Publishing House, 1984). Davidson has given us a very helpful guide to assist grievers as we move through the mourning process. Very important issues are clearly presented and discussed.

Graham, Billy. *Facing Death and the Life After.* (Irving, Tex.: Word Books, 1987). A very readable book which gives many examples of how others have productively dealt with the pain of loss and grief.

James, J. W. and Friedman, R. *The Grief Recovery Handbook.* (New York: Harper-Collins Publishers, Inc., 1998). This little volume offers grievers the specific actions needed to complete the grieving process and to accept loss.

Meyer, Charles. *Surviving Death.* (Mystic, Conn.: Twenty-Third Publications, 1993). Here is a small volume that should be a must on every griever's reading list. Chaplain Meyer combines insights from his many years of counseling grievers and their families with practical information and good humor.

Mitchell, K. R. and Anderson, H. *All Our Losses, All Our Griefs.* (Philadelphia: Westminster Press, 1983). This is an excellent and comprehensive study of the grieving process.

O'Connor, Nancy. *Letting Go with Love: The Grieving Process.* (Tucson, Ariz.: LaMariposa Press, 1997). Kubler-Ross endorses this as a good book that is very readable—a "two thumbs up" book.

Sanders, Catherine M. *Grief, The Morning After: Dealing with Adult Bereavement.* (New York: John Wiley and Sons, Inc., 1999). This is an integrative theory of bereavement that serves as the basis for effective strategic interventions for those suffering with grief. It is an excellent working resource for therapists, social workers, psychiatrists, nurses, grief counselors, and anyone else who is looking for a more comprehensive understanding of the grieving process and its resolution.

Staudacher, Carol. *Beyond Grief.* (Oakland, Calif.: New Harbinger Publications, Inc., 1987). Here is an excellent guide for anyone recovering from the death of a loved one. The author touches many concerns of the grieving person and gives suggestions for coping strategies and nurturing techniques.

Walsh, F. and McGoldrick, M., eds. *Living Beyond Loss: Death in the Family.* (New York: W. W. Norton and Co., 1991). Two experts in the field of family systems edit this volume, which contains a treasure of information focused on families and how they deal with loss.

Worden, W. J. *Grief Counseling and Grief Therapy.* (New York: Springer Publishing Co., 1982). Although this is a handbook for professional grief counselors, it is written in a style that is reader-friendly and contains information that every griever can use.

Grievers are plagued by the haunting question, "Am I alone in my grief experience?" The answer is an emphatic *no*. The Divine Presence is always with us, of course, but there are a multitude of more tangible supports available—online and via more traditional communication channels.

Online resources offer information that addresses specific grief needs. Many Web sites feature a variety of links to other online documents and organizations that offer support to grieving persons and to the family and friends of the bereaved. The sites listed below are simply starting points in the vast network of resources available on the Internet.

www.aarp.org/griefandloss

www.funeral.net/brvres.html

www.compassionatefriends.org

www.geocities.com/ncmb/geo

For those who hesitate to use computers and prefer the U.S. Postal Service and telephone for making connections, the list below offers just a few of the organizations that offer support to bereaved persons.

The Compassionate Friends, Inc.
P.O. Box 3696
Oak Brook, Illinois 60522-3696
(708) 990-0010

This is a somewhat informal organization that has chapters in every state. The organization encourages support groups and publishes books and brochures related to grief and loss. The group is particularly sensitive to the grief needs of parents and siblings.

The Theos Foundation
717 Liberty Avenue
Pittsburgh, Pennsylvania 15222
(412) 471-7779

The name Theos is an acronym signifying the purpose of this organization: They Help Each Other Spiritually. The group provides books and other resources to bereaved persons. One of the foundation's more helpful brochures is titled "Grief Is Not a Sign of Weakness."

The Widowed Person Service
1909 K Street, N.W., Room 580
Washington, D.C. 20049
(202) 728-4370

This organization offers referrals, programs for family adjustment, and counseling for grieving persons or groups. This service provides information on a variety of aspects of loss, including some valuable resources dealing with financial and legal concerns.

The Foundation of Thanatology
630 W. 168th Street
New York, New York 10032
(212) 928-2066

Although this group is organized for professional theology, psychology, health, and social science personnel, its commitment to concerns about mortality and grief make it an excellent and well-used resource.

conclusion

Loss and grief never lose their challenge.
There is no panacea for resolving their pain,
for taking us back to the way things were—
or to the way we think things were—before
our encounter with a personal bereavement.
In order to get a handle on our loss and
grief experiences, we need to remain aware
of what we already know: namely, that
bereavement is a fact of life. It is a universal
experience that is here to stay, and nothing
we can do will alter the fact. We are
brought face to face with this reality each
time we experience the challenge of a significant change in our life.

It has been suggested already that many
different factors influence the intensity and
duration of the grieving process. We are well
aware that each of us carries within us the

effects of our life-experience. We know that our childhood impressions, educational opportunities, social and supportive networks, psychoneurological sensitivity, health history, and spiritual maturity are all among those factors that influence our response to loss and grief.

We also know that our control over these life-events is limited, that our loss-pain is often debilitating, and that we would like to have some measure of control over these events. Too often we feel like passive pawns in this life-game, as if we have little say in these significant changes. We must keep in mind, however, that change itself is a necessary condition for life. To be alive means to be in the flow of God's creative process. High-level well-being is synonymous with change, growth, and development at every level of our existence.

Many of us overlook (or prefer to ignore) how our day-to-day encounters with life's ordinary challenges help to prepare us for our more significant losses. Giving attention to the necessary—and often uncomfortable— routine changes in our lives is not anyone's idea of pleasant musings. And yet, these daily transitions are "little losses" that carry an important—though not always obvious—message. They suggest that the changes taking place in the external world must be matched with changes developing within us. These daily challenges bid us to open ourselves to that uncontrollable creative flow that will eventually bring us to personal and spiritual maturity, to that internal change of attitude that is under our full control.

We are free to accept or reject each challenge; we are not free to sidestep the consequences of that decision. If we opt for acceptance, then we can hope to feel peace and comfort after we have worked through the pain that accompanies change. If we choose to reject reality, then a brief period of denial will probably precede many months—perhaps even years—of ongoing confusion and discomfort. The choice is our own.

If we choose to adopt an attitude of openness to new possibilities, then we will find that gradually our perspective on life and its losses will broaden and deepen, while our values and commitments remain firmly anchored in the truth. As we mature in body, mind, and spirit, we will put away the mind of a child; we will put on the mind of Christ. Indeed, we have a mandate to grow, to pass beyond the myopia of childhood to an adulthood that not only envisions a broader, God-centered perspective, but more particularly, one that sees our losses and grief from a higher level of consciousness and acceptance, from an attitude of Christian expectation and trust.

That choice to accept or reject the reality of loss determines whether we open ourselves to the fullness of life or to the constraints of denial. We are reasonably well acquainted with the painful problems that accompany our loss. Perhaps, however, we are not sufficiently aware of the long-term benefits and blessings that accrue through our understanding and acceptance of loss and grief. The way to acceptance is difficult, but paradoxically, it is also "easy."

Any honest person will acknowledge that during a period of rehabilitation, the demands of physical therapy are most uncomfortable. But a broken leg, for example, will not heal fully unless the pain of therapy is accepted and the tasks for healing are accomplished. In a similar way, spiritual "therapy" calls for an acceptance of our painful loss-changes and of the need to accomplish the healing tasks. Loss and grief tell us that our "broken spirit" needs mending.

In spite of the general discomfort and specific negative feelings associated with the thought of loss and grief, the end results of "loss rehab" are gratifying. Many recovering grievers who have shared their acceptance-of-loss experience report that when their grief work was in process and their recovery neared its completion, a sense of freedom and peace filled their hearts. In taking our grief work seriously, we learn to move into each challenge with greater understanding, sincere acceptance, personal maturity, and the conviction that although the loss, change, and growth process is difficult, our God walks each step of the way with us.

So, the longing of God's people for freedom and peace is not an empty wish. It is the very real experience of those who pass through the fire of grief and come to take seriously their personal and spiritual growth. Living in Christ is a day-to-day happening. It is an awareness that life's truth is beyond—but not contrary to—our human understanding. It is the acceptance of amazing grace that manifests itself even in the losses and griefs of our everyday lives. May we all learn to accept our life-losses and to appreciate the hidden graces and benefits that they bring. And may we come to live in the fullness of God's faithful promise of freedom and peace.

selected bibliography

The annotated resources listed in Section 7 are intended specifically for individuals who are themselves grieving. This bibliography is more comprehensive, featuring a variety of resources for individuals and groups; laity and pastors; grievers, care-givers, and counselors.

Anderson, Herbert and Mitchell, Kenneth. *All Our Losses, All Our Griefs*. Philadelphia: The Westminster Press, 1983.

Anderson, Ray S. *Theology, Death, and Dying*. New York: Basil Blackwell Inc., 1986.

Archer, John. *The Nature of Grief*. London, England: Routledge, 1999.

Bowlby, John. *Loss*. New York: Basic Books, Inc., 1980.

————. *Separation*. New York: Basic Books, Inc., 1973.

Carlozzi, Carl G. *Death and Contemporary Man*. Grand Rapids, Mich.: W. B. Eerdmans Publishing Company, 1968.

Davidson, Glen W. *Understanding Mourning*. Minneapolis: Augsburg Publishing House, 1984.

Deits, Bob. *Life after Loss*. Tucson, Ariz.: Fisher Books, LLC, 2000.

Dudley, William. *Death and Dying*. San Diego: Greenhaven Press, Inc., 1992.

Gordon, David C. *Overcoming the Fear of Death*. Baltimore: Penguin Books, Inc., 1970.

Harvey, John, ed. *Perspectives on Loss: A Sourcebook*. Philadelphia: Brunner/Mazel, 1998.

James, J. W. and Friedman, R. *The Grief Recovery Handbook*. New York: Harper-Collins Publishers, Inc., 1998.

Kung, Hans and Jens, Walter. *Dying with Dignity*. New York: Continuum Publishing Company, 1998.

Lepp, Ignace. *Death and Its Mysteries.* New York: The Macmillan Company, 1968.

Levine, Stephen. *Meeting at the Edge.* New York: Doubleday and Company, Inc., 1984.

———. *Who Dies?* New York: Doubleday and Company, Inc., 1982.

Meyer, Charles. *Surviving Death.* Mystic, Conn.: Twenty-Third Publications, 1993.

Nolen-Hoeksema, S. and Larson, J. *Coping with Loss.* Mahwah, N.J.: Lawrence Erlbaum Associates Publishers, 1999.

Nouwen, Henri. *In Memorium.* Notre Dame, Ind.: Ave Maria Press, 1980.

O'Connor, Nancy. *Letting Go with Love: The Grieving Process.* Tucson, Ariz.: LaMariposa Press, 1997.

Pincus, Lily. *Death and the Family.* New York: Random House, 1976.

Powell, John. *A Reason to Live! A Reason to Die!* Allen, Tex.: Argus Communications, 1975.

Rando, Therese. *Grief, Dying, and Death.* Champaign, Ill.: Research Press Company, 1984.

Sanders, Catherine. *Grief, The Morning After: Dealing with Adult Bereavement.* New York: John Wiley and Sons, Inc., 1999.

Smedes, Lewis. *Forgive and Forget.* San Francisco: Harper and Row Publishers, 1984.

Staudacher, Carol. *Beyond Grief.* Oakland, Calif.: New Harbinger Publications, Inc., 1987.

Stern, E. Mark. *Psychotherapy and the Grieving Patient.* New York: The Haworth Press, 1985.

Stroebe, W. and Stroebe, M. *Bereavement and Health.* New York: Cambridge University Press, 1987.

Tschudin, Verena. *Counseling for Loss and Bereavement.* Philadelphia: Bailliere Tindall, 1997.

Williams, Philip. *When a Loved One Dies.* Minneapolis: Augsburg Publishing House, 1976.

Worden, William. *Grief Counseling and Grief Therapy.* New York: Springer Publishing Company, 1982.